Advanced Speaking Concepts

Also by Stephen Outram...

Books:
Public Speaking: Beyond Fear
Dealers: Buying, Selling & Making Money
There's No Sex in Golf
Life After

Blog & Articles:
stephenoutram.com

Advanced Speaking Concepts

By Stephen Outram

Foreword by Dr. John Thoma

Disclaimer: This product is designed to provide information and motivation to readers. It is sold with the understanding that the publisher is not engaged to render any type of psychological, legal, or any other kind of professional advice. The content of this product is the sole expression and opinion of its author, and not necessarily that of the publisher. No warranties or guarantees are expressed or implied by the publisher's choice to include any of the content in this product. Neither the publisher nor the author shall be liable for any physical, psychological, emotional, financial, or commercial damages, including, but not limited to, special, incidental, consequential or other damages. Our views and rights are the same: You are responsible for your own choices, actions, and results.

Author: Stephen Outram

Date Published: June 1, 2014

ISBN: 978-0-9802927-2-5

Publisher: What Else is Possible?
PO Box 1770, Broadbeach, QLD. 4218. Australia

© 2014 Stephen Outram. All rights reserved. This material may not be reproduced, displayed, modified or distributed without the express prior written permission of the copyright holder. For permission, contact www.stephenoutram.com

Contents

Foreword — 8
By Dr. John Thoma

Preface — 10
Freedom to Create

Introduction — 12
The Adventure Continues

Speak or Die — 15
Unravelling the Myth

Vulnerability — 18
No Barriers

Nerves — 26
Potent Energy

Speaking to the Future — 30
10 Years Out

Be the Speaker — 35
Swapping Roles

Orchestrate — 40
Opening doorways

Working with Masters — 48
Receiving Contribution

Exclusion — 53
What Can You Add?

Applause — 58
A Beginning

About The Author   63
Biography

Related Books   65
Public Speaking: Beyond Fear

Foreword

By Dr. John Thoma

The coin spun in the air and landed on a glass table and I said, "Heads!"

But a little voice under the table squeaked, "No, it's Tails." Just then 5 year old Jenny walked by and reported, "Nope, I see Edges." Three people, three stories and three "truths." Who's right? What if it's just your point of view that creates your reality? What else is possible if you look from another point of view? This question is the source of Stephen's book.

Looking beyond contemporary ideas about public speaking Stephen explores speaking from totally different points of view that are challenging, transforming and refreshing. He turns conventional wisdom upside down and shows you how to change anxiety into excitement and how to use hidden issues to your advantage.

Stephen invites you to explore new ways to communicate with your audience in a compelling and memorable way so they really grasp your message. How exciting could your speaking career be if you turned your fear of public speaking and vulnerability into a playful adventure of communicating with your audience? And how much fun speaking are you willing to have?

Stephen's writing style is conversational, inviting and engaging. I had a sense while reading his book that we were often having a friendly chat. His thoughts were illuminating and challenged me to question widely held beliefs about public speaking. His ideas offer generative, expansive and most importantly *living tools* for enhancing any speakers' potential to engage an audience.

I am delighted to have new tools, to communicate more effectively with people on a daily basis. That is Stephen's greatest gift for me.

Dr. John Thoma.
Doctor of Philosophy (PhD), Chemistry & Biochemistry. Former Professor of Chemistry & Biochemistry at University of Arkansas and Assistant Professor of Chemistry Indiana University; and the author of over 80 scientific publications, reviews and book chapters.

Preface

Freedom to Create

This is my second book on the topic of public speaking. The first, *Public Speaking: Beyond Fear*, was written in 2006 and updated in 2014. It has been, not only personally rewarding to explore public speaking more fully, but somewhat cathartic at the same time.

I have come to realize that while some things do come to an end and we move on, others are more intricately woven into our lives. Public speaking and the expanding freedom to express and create has been, and continues to be, an unfolding adventure for me…one that I cherish.

When I was younger, I had hoped that one day I would be free of the anxiety of speaking to groups. But I find now that it is more to do with *being free to create*, with groups, in relationships, writing or whatever I choose.

While I was concentrating on fixing my speaking issues, they turned out to be symptoms, not causes. Symptoms can be your best friend; the most intense and challenging clues pointing to hidden doorways and guiding you through the matrix of your unconsciousness.

I'm well pleased with this book. It compliments and adds to its predecessor, while presenting some larger concepts that you may like to explore and integrate with your own speaking or performances. These are not intended to be answers to problems or fixed methods on how to do something, but nutrition for your own work that may act as a catalyst for you creating something even greater.

Life is an adventure; be curious, ask questions, explore, enjoy and continue seeking ever-greater freedom to create your life and living.

Warm Regards,
Stephen Outram

Stephen Outram

Introduction

The Adventure Continues

Groups of people; societies can hold certain viewpoints very strongly, however, when those views are turned around by 180 degrees and examined, a different perspective is possible. Take "vulnerability" for example, it's a popular and widely held view that if you are vulnerable then you are weak; open to attack.

> "...at the time, I believed vulnerability was a liability. I was okay with being the dragon lady. It was safe. And under that façade, no one knew how terrified I actually was. So I wore that armor as if my life depended on it."— Wendy Miyake, author and teacher.

In fact, one of my favorite online sources[1] describes vulnerability as being from the Latin word vulnerare "to wound, hurt, injure, maim." Hmm, not very nice.

180 degrees! The armor we wear and the barriers we erect to protect ourselves also work really well in keeping everything else out. For example, we may make ourselves invulnerable to receiving money, applause, awareness, praise, valuable feedback, audience signals or having fun and ease with our speaking. Have we judged

---

1   The Online Dictionary of Etymology

vulnerability harshly, perhaps based on someone else's experience of it? Can vulnerability actually work for you; allowing something new; something different with public speaking and performance?

Likewise, "manipulation" is generally thought to be deceitful, immoral and sometimes evil. But without it how would you get your kids to go to bed on time, lower someone's defences to be able to assist them, or allow your audience to see choices that they may not otherwise have been aware of?

> "When life gives you lemons, manipulate the lemon salesman."—Lifehacker

How many things have we decided are bad to use or wrong to use that can actually work very well for a speaker?

Who would have thought that by choosing to include certain people, you can exclude a large portion of your audience? Or that nerves are a potent energy that many speakers try to quell, rather than "amping" them up and using nerves to enhance a performance? How many things do speakers exclude or reject that are some of the most dynamic skills and tools available?

I've observed many speakers; our politicians for example, using the same, worn techniques that have been employed for decades, corporate CEOs nervously hiding behind lecterns at shareholder meetings, actors lost without their lines when receiving an award and school children reciting learned passages like parrots. Is that really what public speaking is about? Is it time for a fresh look at public speaking? What are we continuing to perpetrate with the old that can be something different with a new, fresh perspective?

I recall someone saying of actor Robert Wagner, who I recall from the 1970s TV series "It Takes a Thief," that he was the last actor of his kind (they were referring to his style of acting). What if you were the *first* speaker of your kind? What if the way you create speaking is fresh, new and different? And are you the only one who can do that…the only one who can speak as you?

Speak or Die

Unravelling the Myth

There is a plethora of similar information citing that, apparently, a large number of us would rather die than get up and speak in front of a group of people.

An Internet search on Google reveals that just about anyone with a book or course, related to public speaking, uses this as a sensationalist marketing device and I question if any of these people have bothered to verify or even to understand it.

With so many people spreading the die/speak message and giving it energy, it can take on a life-force of its own and become widely accepted, as true. Well, I'm questioning it. Will you?

Does it make any sense to you that many of us—nearly half the population—would rather die than talk to a group of people? I mean...really? Imagine that I have a big gun pointed at you and I say, "Okay! A bullet in the head or you get up on that stage and say a few words." With those as my only two choices, I would be heading for the stage. How about you?

Many authors and experts cite *The Book of Lists* as the primary source for this die/speak phenomenon. This is incorrect. R. H. Bruskin Associates conducted a survey in 1973 (over 40 years ago) and asked respondents to pick from a list of 14 topics. Public speaking rated highly—at over 40%—as something they had some level of fear about. A more recent 2001 Gallop Poll, based on 20 topics, indicates that "Animals and Bugs" are top of the list. Go figure.

> "I am aware of [an] Australian survey. It is one of the silliest ones around because both the newspaper article and press release only refer to public speaking and death."—Richard I. Garber 2011, Joyful Public Speaking Blog.

Clearly, the information has been manipulated to sensationalize, market and benefit those with a vested interest.

I ask you now, please, can we put this one to bed? Can we let go of a 40 plus year old survey, (and everything that has been fabricated on top of it) and allow it to go to the final resting place of misused old surveys…in peace.

Thank you! What else is possible?

My priority in bringing this up is not to dismiss the fear that people have of public speaking, but to begin dissipating the energy that gets locked-up in something when we buy into the sensation of it as real and true

How much fear do we actually create when we buy into other people's stories and viewpoints and make them ours? What could be different if you don't accept the story that public speaking is something to be feared?

Is it possible that your fear is based on someone else's fear and they got that from someone else and so on?

How much of the fear you have associated with public speaking is actually yours? Any of it? And if it is not your fear, then what is this energy that you notice when you get up to speak? More on that in another chapter.

Public speaking is simply public speaking and you are you; what can you create with public speaking that you have never before considered possible?

Stephen Outram

Vulnerability

No Barriers

Being vulnerable is having no barriers up. It is the barriers you put up, in defence, that prevent you connecting-with and receiving-from your audience. Vulnerability is one of the most inclusive and compelling experiences an audience can have, yet few speakers are willing to be the invitation that creates this being possible.

> "Staying vulnerable is a risk we have to take if we want to experience connection." Professor, researcher and author Brené Brown.

Barriers are what you use to establish and maintain a comfortable distance between you and what you have decided is unpleasant or even dangerous. Those decisions may have been taken based on what you learned from a trusted few. In the story overleaf, a child learns from her mother that crowds are dangerous and hides in her skirts; a flimsy barrier.

Barriers can take many forms, a lectern or a guitar for example, but the ones that are most difficult to change are the ones you are not aware of. I'm not saying that lecterns or guitars should not be used, but if you are using them as a defence and don't know it, then your ability to be vulnerable is affected.

In a singing competition, The Voice, that I watched on television, Celia Pavey performed with an acoustic guitar. After several rounds she was asked to sing a song without using the instrument. She began, obviously uncomfortable, but there was a point in the song when she connected with the music and forgot all about not having a shield. The change was remarkable and the audience immediately responded enthusiastically, acknowledging her. When she gave up the protection, her audience could more fully connect with her and contribute.

While I was President of Gold Coast Toastmasters Club, a new member was giving his third speech. Head down, he began reading from papers on the lectern. After a few minutes, he came to the part of the speech that he knew about; the core of the topic. He looked up from the print and began speaking in a very different way, with surety and presence. With his written speech no longer the barrier he was using to separate from the audience, he went on to deliver a very credible and engaging talk. And now, many years later, I still remember that he spoke about the destruction of forests to clear land for housing. His speech became memorable to me.

How are barriers created and what might they look like?

> Once upon a time, when you were very young, you were walking happily with your mother. She turned into a busy street and suddenly grasped your hand. There were a lot of people around you as you looked up from your three foot high perspective. Mum leant down and told you to stay very close and, as you were highly sensitive to her emotions, you

knew she was nervous; the crowd scared her. In that moment you *decided* that crowds must be a very bad thing, to scare your mother so, and you too became scared and hid behind her skirts.

Today, perhaps some 20 or 30 years later, that decision is still in place though you no longer remember making it. You always feel nervous when confronted by a crowd and have no idea why. Every time you get that feeling, you automatically begin putting up energetic barriers (skirts) to defend against the crowd, without knowing why. And what else have you created, based on that foundational decision, that still affects you today?

Barriers are used to defend and they are a choice we make each time we raise them. You will notice your barriers when someone assails them, for example, a pushy sales person, an annoyingly persistent child or someone who is sexually interested in you. When someone steps into your "personal space" or tests your barriers, you have several choices:

- Retreat, to maintain your comfortable distance

- Intensify the energy of your barrier, hoping they will notice and back off

- Fight verbally or physically in an attempt to drive them away

- Push all of your barriers down

Retreat could be seen as a sign of weakness, intensify or fight may result in stronger attacks, but pushing down all of your barriers will likely confuse and disarm the person because there is no longer anything for them to

Advanced Speaking Concepts

push against. More on that in a moment.

As you are reading this, take notice of what's going on inside your head right now and you may gain some insight about foundational decisions that you have taken, in the past, justifying the barriers you raise now.

We use many different barriers to defend against imaginary enemies, often without knowing why. And you always have the choice to raise these barriers, but what we are looking for here is another choice, a different choice that you can make.

> What barriers are no longer required if, rather than fear-of-crowds, you chose ease-of-crowds or fun-of-crowds?

To be able to have different choices you must first become aware-of and acknowledge when you do put up barriers. If you are unconscious of a choice that you make, i.e. running on autopilot, then you cannot choose differently. When you are aware of a barrier then you can choose to push it down. How do you push a barrier down? You do it the same way as you raise them, you just do it! Ask yourself, "Have I got any barriers up here?" and if you have then push them down.

If you have been using barriers in your defence, then pushing them down and having no barriers presents additional, different possibilities. More possibilities gives you greater choice, which allows you to create something different. **Choice creates.** The two areas that we will cover in this chapter are:

1. Connection

2. Perceiving

Connection

Connection is possible and begins when people lower their barriers to each other. If you have your barriers up, and they do too, then connection is not possible.

Connection is a joining; a trusting where the audience allows *you* to take them into your care. It is similar to the way a small child *chooses* to hold your hand rather than you using superior size and strength to force them, often resulting in the child resisting and fighting you.

You will hear performers, comedians, speakers and the like talk about "building rapport" or "breaking the ice" these are what a speaker does to try and get through barriers and create connection. "Breaking" down barriers can be a lot of work.

> "Comedian Bernie McGrenahan is using laughter to break the ice on Fort Hood [United States military post] on this Suicide Prevention Day. After 30 minutes of stand-up comedy, he has the soldiers' attention. Then he begins sharing his powerful story about the day his 19 year old brother killed himself, forever changing the lives of everyone around him."— Sophia Stamas, KCEN TV.

Make this easier by leading and consciously pushing down your own barriers. When *you* have no barriers, there is nothing for your audience to defend against and their own barriers begin to dissolve. With no barriers, a wonderful thing happens…most people come off defence and can relax. It is then that you and what you have to say can be more easily received.

Some years ago I worked with a company that made regular presentations designed to educate audiences about its products. David was often the host, opening the event and introducing various speakers.

When he spoke to the group his voice would shake and often a glossy sheen appeared on his forehead. David never defended his nervousness nor did he deny it; occasionally he joked about it. His vulnerability with this allowed audiences to connect, trust him and receive what he said. Despite his "imperfect" style, he was always warmly received and became very successful. Not trying to hide the obvious or garner sympathy, David simply got on with the job.

Connection allows the distance between you and another person to seemingly disappear. When you join with the audience, then the stage, podium and distance no longer separate you. Your speech can become a conversation, which is inclusive, compelling and invites contribution.

Perceiving

Perceiving is having a sense of all the information that is available to you. It becomes possible when you do not block anything by putting up barriers and is enhanced when you create connection. You can be aware of many things via the sensorial capacities of your body and in addition, you can be sensitive to less tangible, energetic information such as anger, thought or excitement. For example:

Have you walked into a room and instantly been aware that someone is furious, or telephoned a friend who picked-up and said, "Wow! I was just about to call you"? In those situations, were you *perceiving* information beyond your body's five senses?

A friend of mine, who was visiting in my area and wanted to see me, asked himself, "Where will I find Stephen?" A few minutes later he walked into a coffee shop where I was reading the paper.

When you step up on stage, and before that, you can perceive; be aware of your audience. Are they excited, expectant, neutral, angry… what information are they sending that you can receive and be aware of?

Perceiving is a wonderful capacity speakers can develop, as it allows them to anticipate and provide what is required; for example, they can change the opening, their words, volume or intensity to better handle what's-up for their audience.

Around 2002, I watched a DVD of *Conversations With God* author Neale Donald Walsch, speaking to a large audience. Walsch was introduced and walked out onto the stage where he turned and looked to the audience, in total silence, for about a minute. Then he said a single sentence consisting of just six words that many people probably remembered for a long time afterwards, "Ladies and Gentlemen, God needs you."

After speaking those six words he was quiet again for several moments, allowing us to receive what he had said. It was a captivating opening. When he spoke again, everyone leaned forward to hear what else he had to say to them.

Was Walsch aware of the audience's excitement and did he give them a minute to settle down and connect?

Did he acknowledge the audience in that long minute's silence and quietly say, "Hello. I see you"? Did he push down his barriers and simply perceive them? Was he vulnerable?

Being Vulnerable

Why do many people enjoy picking up a baby or young animal for a cuddle? Because a baby does not judge, has no barriers up and is totally vulnerable. Vulnerability is an invitation like no other; it says, "Hi! I see you. Who are you? Come and play."

What could be different if you were the inclusive, compelling invitation to your audience that says, "Hi! I see you. Who are you? Come and play?"

Stephen Outram

Nerves

Potent Energy

What speakers refer to as "nerves" can be a potent energy used to their advantage or disadvantage. When nerves are mastered they can work for you, rather than you using them against you. In addition, it has been shown that widely accepted "coping" techniques can actually work against a speaker (emphasis is mine).

> "Individuals often feel anxious in anticipation of tasks such as speaking in public or meeting with a boss. I find that an overwhelming majority of people believe trying to calm down is the best way to cope with pre-performance anxiety.
>
> However, across several studies involving karaoke singing, public speaking and math performance, I investigate an alternative strategy: reappraising anxiety as excitement. Compared with those who attempt to calm down, **individuals who reappraise their anxious arousal as excitement feel more excited and perform better.**"—Alison Wood Brooks, Harvard Business School.

Many professional and experienced artists, for example, Barbra Streisand, Frank Sinatra and Ella Fitzgerald have spoken about experiencing intense nerves before

Advanced Speaking Concepts

every show. Yet, they can go on stage and create extraordinary performances.

> "I'm very shy, and I shy away from people. But the moment I hit the stage, it's a different feeling. I get nerve from somewhere; maybe it's because it's something I love to do."—Ella Fitzgerald, singer, performer.

Some people are disabled by their nerves. This "disability" can be a symptom of something else, though it is treated or blamed as the cause. The something else; the cause, is totally invisible behind the emotional distraction that is created using nerves. They use the energy of nerves to disable them, often, based on a point of view that they are not aware of. It is the viewpoint that is the underlying cause, which needs to be handled.

> "Your point of view creates your reality, it is not your reality that creates your point of view."— Dr. Dain Heer, author, presenter.

What does using nerves to disable look like and how might that come about? Let's imagine that, in your very early teens, you agreed to participate in your school's Annual Ball. It was traditional to have students performing different acts creating a variety show and you are asked to do a ten minute stand-up comedy routine.

You find some good jokes and decide to tell an embarrassing story about your Mum, as the big finish. You want this to be a big surprise so you don't tell anyone or use the material in rehearsals.

The day of the Annual Ball arrives and soon it is your

turn to go on stage. You tell your jokes, get some laughs and the act seems to be going well. As the last few minutes approach you are feeling really confident and launch into the big surprise. You don't notice how quiet the audience has become as you progress the tale and when you pop the punch line…no one laughs and it is dead quiet. The only sound you hear is your Mum's gasp of horror and the drumming of her heels as she dashes for the door; too embarrassed and upset to stay. Oops!

When you get home, your Dad is furious with you and Mum is in her bedroom crying. You realise what you have done, and in that moment vow to never ever get on stage again and hurt someone as you have hurt your Mum. It seems there is nothing you can do or say to make things better and despondently you head on up to the seclusion of your room.

Please note, "never ever" is a very long time. You can see that with that vow in place, speaking in groups is going to be really difficult, as now, some years later, you will probably remember the event but have forgotten the vow you took. How much energy did you bind into that powerful, now hidden vow that is the root cause driving you to use nerves to disable you as a speaker? And what else have you created on top of it? Phew!

Nerves are an energy that you have available to you. Nerves are where you begin expanding the energy that you normally function from, to be intense enough or big enough to connect-with and be noticed-by a large group of people. It's where you energise every cell in your body and all of your molecules begin clanging together.

Advanced Speaking Concepts

When you are chatting with a friend it is not necessary to be super intense, in fact, that can be annoying.
But when you are speaking to ten, one hundred or a thousand people, it takes more energy.

You may have seen singers competing in *Voice America*, *The Voice* and other similar television shows. Some contestants sing well, but they seem meek and lackluster. Others give it everything they've got! They are intense; dynamic and you are enthralled by their performance. Later, when they are interviewed, they exclaim, "I feel amazing!" and no wonder when they have that much energy flowing through their body.

This second group of singers use nervous energy to their advantage. They don't call it nerves or nervous; it is, as Ella Fitzgerald said "I get nerve…" and it is the energy that they be when they perform. It is **the nerve of you to be intense, dynamic and different** that can set you apart from everyone else. Are your molecules clanging together yet?

> Where or from-whom did you buy into the idea that "nerves" are a bad thing?

When you get over your fixed views and stop judging nerves as a bad thing, then you have a different choice. You have the possibility of using a potent energy— the nerve of you—to your advantage, to enhance and intensify you and your performance beyond what you have previously considered possible.

You may be able to reach out farther and connect with more people than ever before, and you may even be able to reach out into the future…but that is another chapter.

Stephen Outram

Speaking to the Future

10 Years Out

Your speeches and presentations can reach out into the future if you create them that way, but when you speak for just now, then your words and their energy will have a limited life-span.

When Dr. Martin Luther King gave his speech "I Have a Dream" in 1963, he was creating something that would live for a very long time. He was speaking for the greater freedom of people referred to as "Negro" and he wanted their freedom to endure. Even today, 40 years later, when I listen-to or read "I Have a Dream," I am aware of the energy that it still has and will continue to have until the job that Dr. King gave it is fully done.

There are many examples where people have spoken words that have contributed to changing something or someone and it has continued to have an effect for many years on; even beyond the speaker's lifetime. A few examples:

Winston Churchill, the British Prime Minister's "We Shall Fight on the Beaches" was given in parliament during World War 2.

> "We shall go on to the end, we shall fight in France, we shall fight on the seas and oceans, we shall fight with growing confidence and growing

> strength in the air, we shall defend our island, whatever the cost may be, we shall fight on the beaches, we shall fight on the landing grounds, we shall fight in the fields and in the streets, we shall fight in the hills; we shall never surrender..."

John F Kennedy's Inaugural Address delivered in 1961.

> "And so, my fellow Americans, ask not what your country can do for you; ask what you can do for your country. My fellow citizens of the world, ask not what America will do for you, but what together we can do for the freedom of man."

In 1977 Diana, Princess of Wales brought attention to the horror of land mines.

> "For the mine is a stealthy killer. Long after conflict is ended, its innocent victims die or are wounded singly, in countries of which we hear little. Their lonely fate is never reported."

United States actor Kevin Spacey's more recent 2010 motivational talk with students.

> "I watch a lot of young people meandering around without any idea about why they're doing what they're doing. I mean...to want and to be ambitious, and to want to be successful is not enough; that's just desire. To know what you want. To understand why you're doing it. To dedicate every breath in your body to achieve. If you feel you have something to give, if you feel that your particular talent is worth developing, is worth caring for, then there is nothing you can't achieve."

Spacey's two minute clip was viewed over 190,000 times in three years on [1]YouTube. And what he said will reach people far into the future because he didn't limit his audience to the students in the room; he spoke-to and beyond present time. That is how classics are created, where the words, songs, books or movies have such a dynamic life force that they span generations. Here are some recent comments about the 2010 video:

> 2014 March, "Great video, very inspirational."
> 2013 October, "Favorite speech."
> 2013 August, "Kevin Spacey shares some amazing words."
> 2013 July, "Great speech!"
> 2013 April, "This is amazing."
> 2013 April, "Frankly, I wasn't expecting this. Excellent!"

How do you speak to the future?

For some, connecting to the future may seem like a weird thing to do; will you suspend your own disbelief and do it anyway? You may never see the result of your work but in doing this you can create a possibility, for someone else, that can not be possible without you. Kevin Spacey may never know the effects of his video, but those who viewed it many years later and were inspired, do.

1. First of all, you must be aware of the possibility; that speaking to the future is possible and then choose it. **Choice creates.**

2. Acknowledge that you can create beyond the apparent limitations of time and that you do have

---

1   Search youtube.com: kevin spacey motivational speech

access to the future.

3. Then, before your presentations, expand-out into the future and connect with all of the people that are looking for you and the information that you have for them.

As you do this more and more and with each presentation that you give, you begin to build the muscle. You will become aware that your audience is not only the five, fifty or five hundred people in front of you; it is becoming vastly bigger.

There is no proof or method of measurement I can give you here except to say that if you do this, there will be a change and you will know! Every talk you give can be more expansive and greater than before. There will be no reason to judge you inadequate or a failure because your group is too small as you will always be talking to audiences beyond (and including) those you see.

It is a similar experience to speaking to a large group (imagine thousands of people in a darkened football stadium), where the only lights are from the stage on which you stand. The first few rows of people are illuminated, yet you know that far out in the darkness there are thousands more listening to your every word.

A television presenter may not have even one person as their live audience but they know, beyond the camera lense, they are speaking with tens of thousands of people.

An actor or singer, recording in a studio, may have only the technical staff watching them but they are creating their movie or song for the thousands who will enjoy it in the future.

> Who could you be speaking with, beyond the room you are in, beyond the audience you are facing and beyond time, if you include the future audience that is seeking you?
>
> What job, task or target can you give your presentations that will allow them to continue expanding out into the future, to accomplish far more than you can even imagine?

Is there a future that you would like to see in the world and have you been whispering to it? I wonder what might show up if you reached out, connected with it and pulled it towards you now.

Be the Speaker

Swapping Roles

Changing your role during a presentation, can confuse an audience and may not create what you desire. Following are two real-life stories that illustrate different approaches to speaking and sales.

One

In the late 1990s I went to several seminars presented by USA born Kurak Ashley, which I enjoyed. He was humorous, had great information and used a variety of engaging examples and stories to exemplify his message. It was at one of Ashley's events that I walked, barefoot, over red-hot coals. That was cool!

> Ashley had scheduled an evening event at Surfers Paradise on Queensland's Gold Coast, near to where I lived. I arrived early to register, and the lobby was already packed with people eager to see the popular presenter. At 6:30pm the auditorium doors swung open and amidst the buzz of excited voices, people found their seats and were finally ready.
>
> The presenter came on stage and began with a high energy delivery of concepts and tools—he was pumped, we were pumped and the show was great. About 60 minutes in we took a 15 minute

refreshment break and then continued. Ashley did another 30 minutes and then said that he was going to talk about some of his products. It was sales time.

I watched with fading interest as this dynamic presenter changed roles and became an enthusiastic sales person. He showed various packages—books, CDs, DVDs—and also explained about how we could sign up for his new program with easy monthly payments and, of course, a special discount if we bought on the night.

By the time he had finished selling his product range, most of the energy that he had generated in the room, with his audience, had dissipated. His final 30-40 minutes seemed lackluster; an anticlimax. He worked very hard to pick it up again but without great success.

By having a sales session during his talk, Ashley sought to capitalise on the high energy he had created; his audience was enthusiastic and excited. But by continuing with his presentation, no one could take the action of purchasing, and the energy and their interest waned.

It was just one night and not a career breaker; I know that he continued to present his seminars in the years following, several of which I attended.

Two
In the late 1990s I attended a Sunday afternoon seminar with Dr. John Demartini at the Brisbane Convention Centre, Queensland. I had gone with some friends and we were looking forward to the presentation

Advanced Speaking Concepts

as none of us had seen Demartini before.

At the appointed start time a well presented man walked on stage and introduced himself as the speaker's manager. He gave us a brief summary of the treat that was in store for us, touched on some of Dr. Demartini's notable achievements and then roused us to applause as he called the speaker. The Doctor came on-stage and began what developed into a terrific afternoon.

Around mid-afternoon we all took a break for tea and cakes. Later, the manager called us back to our seats and took 15 or so minutes to pitch Demartini's upcoming 3 day seminar and books. Again, he asked for our applause and called the Doctor back on stage for the second half of his presentation.

When Demartini finished, his manager was quickly on-stage and applauding with us. As the speaker retired from the stage his manager directed and lead us to the product displays and sales team.

I enjoyed Demartini's seminar very much. He was always the charismatic presenter and never the sales person. Cleverly, he had hired a talented professional to do that job.

What can we learn from these two stories?

Your Team
Make sure you have people in your team who can do what is required to give you the space to be the speaker and contribute to creating a great experience for your audience. Often, people are happy to work for you in exchange for the seminar or perhaps a private session

with you, and if you pay them it will be well worth the ease it creates for you.

I recall giving a seminar on the topic of technology and the Internet. There was some technology that I had to setup, which would record the event; I was also collecting at-the-door fees. Just before start time, I hurried over to the recording desk to switch everything on and then stepped up on stage. I checked that the microphones were working, "Test. Test." and began. The seminar went well but when I checked the recording two hours later, nothing had been captured at all! I was planning on selling the audios after the event. It was a costly mistake.

If you are the one checking people in and collecting their money or serving the refreshments during break, it can take-away from you being the speaker. In addition, it can demean how your audience perceives you—are you the speaker or the tea lady? **You are the speaker… be that with every fibre of your being!**

Selling from the Stage

There is a technique called selling from the stage and some speakers can do it very well. Seminars of this type are designed specifically to sell products. The idea is to manipulate the audience into having a very strong desire for the product and making them a special one-time offer that's hard to resist.

When you create the energy that connects your audience with products that you have for sale, make sure they can act immediately. Consider how the parts of your talk go together to allow a space for your audience to buy.

Announce It

If you choose to be the salesman, or other roles during your event then announce it so that everyone is clear about what is happening. "I'm changing roles now and will be a salesman for 15 minutes while I talk about some of my products." Be confident when you move to a new role and make no apology. And when you are done selling, announce that the sales are done and you are now going to continue as speaker.

Be open with your audience and they will appreciate it. If you are having some other people up on-stage then announce it. A presenter I know will have some of his people on-stage to provide certain information; he says, "We are going to have some announcements now." And he stays on the stage to make sure the audience pays attention, and often adds to the information and supports his people.

In all of this, you have to look at what you would like to create with your speaking events and the audiences you have, and where your talents lie in best achieving your targets. Be willing to have the contribution of others, and to pay for that. It may create more for you than you realize.

Stephen Outram

Orchestrate

Opening doorways

You do not create in isolation. It is both speaker *and* audience that create the speech; both have their parts to play that, as a whole, contribute to the outcome. As a speaker, the point of focus, you are the leader and if you do not lead then your audience will wander-off and be lost to you.

As a speaker, one of the tools available is to orchestrate; the speaker manipulates to get the audience more fully connected with what is being talked about or presented. In a similar way, a conductor works-with and combines elements of his orchestra to create a symphony; his choice of arrangement affects the music that is produced.

> "I think it's a very important collaboration between the conductor and the orchestra - especially when the conductor is one more member of the orchestra in the way that you are leading, but also respecting, feeling and building the same way for all the players to understand the music."—Gustavo Dudamel

An orchestra knows what its job is, as does an audience. Audiences are trained from a very young age, for example, when Mom began talking or singing to her baby to get its attention, groups of young children go to school to sit before a teacher and employees work for their boss. Audiences already know what their job is but often, speakers do not.

> "What is it about a conductor like Deral Johnson that allows real music making to happen at nearly every rehearsal and creates performances that become lifetime memories for singers and audiences alike? How does this conductor bridge the gap between technique and getting so meaningfully 'beyond the notes'?"— Victoria Meredith, from *The Conductor as Catalyst*.

Deral Johnson is well known for moving the people in his choirs around during rehearsals, "…to keep them alive and thinking…for them to hear all types of other sounds in the choir." Rearranging the way people are seated is an example of orchestration. It is where the speaker manipulates the audience to some effect. There are many tools and techniques available to be used, which can be learned by watching experienced speakers objectively, reading famous speeches, attending workshops, etc. Using these appropriately can create extraordinary results.

In a practical sense, orchestration may seem to be about moving people around and playing with an audience in various ways, but there is more to be aware-of than just technique and method. Having a sense of the effect you are going to create, with the choices you make, can be a useful capacity.

In my twenties I recall going to a seminar where the

presenter singled me out to front the audience and lead a free-form exercise activity. I did not want to appear weak and went to the front of the room as asked. I began to do some star jumps but was so nervous I could only think of two exercises to do, and alternated between them. Eventually the presenter stopped us all, thanked me and I returned to my seat. I was highly embarrassed by the whole thing. After the seminar he came to find me and apologized. His results could have been much better if he had asked for someone who was "willing" to do the task.

If you are unwilling to manipulate or are unaware of your audience's unwillingness to be manipulated, then orchestration can work against you. There are two key parts to orchestration. The willingness of:

1. The speaker to orchestrate

2. The audience to be manipulated

It is the speaker that facilitates both of these being possible.

The Speaker Orchestrating

Is it your view that orchestration; manipulation is wrong or bad? If it is, then you will be unwilling to employ this tool and use it to assist you in influencing an audience.

Words alone[1], even when coupled with a pretty face, are not enough. It seems a contradiction to take a strong

---

1 In my other book, *Public Speaking: Beyond Fear*, I describe an audience that was only able to recall a few words from a short, 3 minute speech.

stand on manipulation as an adult, when as a kid you were probably using it regularly, and with some skill.

> "Kids manipulate their parents. It's part of their normal routine. They learn to use their charms and strengths to get their way and negotiate more power in the family."— James Lehman, Behavioral Therapist.

Would it be easier, to consider manipulation as a tool that can facilitate people in your audiences having access to choices they would not normally allow themselves?

In his seminars, Dr. Dain Heer will invite various members of the audience to join him on stage, where he can work directly with them. With some, there is hesitation as the person can be reluctant to dismember from the safety of the audience. He orchestrates by first inviting someone that he knows is willing, or seems less powerful such as a child, which can crack open the doorway for those who would like to choose but are afraid.

At one event I attended, he asked a young girl who declined. He smiled and gently said, "That's fine." Dr. Heer was showing the girl and audience that they all had a choice; he would not force them to accept. He invited another person who accepted and continued.

Later, he asked the young girl once again. This time she said, "Yes!" went up on stage and sat with him. They talked, laughed, giggled, played and had a lot of fun. When the session was finished, she talked confidently with the audience as if she had been doing it her whole life.

During the morning she had watched Dr. Heer work with other people and could see that there was nothing to fear; the young girl was able to trust him and accept his invitation. Her choice also assisted those who were still unsure.

Please note, it takes tremendous courage for the timid to choose beyond their fear. The choice they make can facilitate many others in choosing too.

Audiences Being Manipulated
Audiences know, at some level, when they are being orchestrated. Parents manipulate their children while their children manipulate them. We all play the game.

> "Nobody likes to feel manipulated and usually people do experience a sense of being manipulated when it happens."— Dr. Susan Rutherford, Clinical Psychologist

The question is, will your audience allow you to orchestrate them or will they resist? It is the speaker that can swing this one way or the other. Here are three things to consider when orchestrating an audience:

1. You must have no vestment in the outcome. Your desire; your need to be successful and create the outcome you want is all about you. It is self motivated, selfish and audiences will sense it and resist you dynamically. You must be willing to allow them to choose, what they choose and when they choose it; you can only present the choices.

2. Be open; vulnerable and tell the audience you are

Advanced Speaking Concepts

manipulating them, and make it fun. Presenter Gary Douglas often demands his audience to "not" do something. Then he laughs and explains that many people will resist when told to "do" something, but are much more likely to do what they are denied. It always gets a laugh and is very effective.

3. Take note of what works and what doesn't. Sometimes you may tell a joke and get little response; another time an audience will laugh unexpectedly while you're speaking. What you think will be funny to an audience may never work; get rid of it. Work at collecting all those moments when you did get laughter and use them again. Be aware of and use what works rather than trying to fix what doesn't.

A feature of Dr. Heer's classes is working closely with people on stage; it's part of how he orchestrates and changes the energy in the room by arranging his audience. Though not everyone gets on stage, Dr. Heer's vulnerability and willingness to share the platform rather than use it as a barrier is very compelling.

Some speakers orchestrate by excluding their audience. You will see this with politicians, who read off prepared speeches, which discourage interjection and questions. Even when questioned, politicians do not answer directly and talk around the question. These are skilful manipulations and as a result, politicians are rarely trusted and audiences do not expect to be included.

During Parliament, in Westminster systems of Government, there is a segment known as "Question Time" where members of the house can ask each other questions. The most numerous complaint is, "The speaker is off-topic and will they please address the question!" Good luck with that!

Orchestration is a tool that speakers can use to get their audiences connected with what is being talked about or presented. You, as a speaker, can open the doorway to possibilities that they may not have been aware of before, but you cannot force people to walk through that door. Even if you can clearly see what is required, you cannot choose it for someone else. To have that possibility, as their own, *they* must choose it otherwise it will be borrowed from you; something that is borrowed always comes with an implied return.

During a one day public speaking class I gave in Queensland, Australia there was a woman who was deeply fearful. She sat in the back rows partially hidden behind a larger person. It would have been unkind to bring her to the front, "to face her fears" as some other teachers may have demanded.

I worked my class and waited patiently for five hours until I knew that she was ready and then invited her to join me. My manipulation was to make her contribution greater than her fear. I asked for permission to facilitate her and explained that this work would create a change not only for her, but for every other person in the room. I said that I had chosen her because I knew she was strong enough to handle it. She rose off her chair without hesitating and came to stand next to me in front of the group. I placed her hand in mine and, with her heart beating like a bass drum, we did the work. She was terrific.

Often, it is the timid that are the most courageous as their leap to freedom is so much greater than that of the seasoned warrior.

To manipulate for self gain, out of self interest or when functioning from need will be resisted dynamically by an audience or a single person. Such work creates a distinct energy that many people will detect and raise barriers against. To orchestrate, without a vested interested in the outcome, with appropriate humour, using what works and functioning from a genuine desire to connect your audience with new possibilities is a much larger and grander work, for a speaker.

Orchestration is a potent skill to master. What can you create with it?

Stephen Outram

Working with Masters

Receiving Contribution

When you choose to be a speaker, a strange thing happens, you gain access to information that you weren't aware of before.

Have you ever noticed that when you buy a new car, suddenly you see all of those cars that are similar to yours? They were on the road before but you were not aware of them. Something changes when you choose.

> What else do you have available to you that a new choice can reveal?

As I am the author of this book, it appears that I am the sole creator but that would be a mistaken assumption. When I began, I asked for assistance from the Masters. I'm not referring to "spiritual" masters that some people like to talk with, but to those people who have mastered speaking.

Some are alive today and some are without bodies I know a few of their names—Dr. Martin Luther King Jr., Winston Churchill, Bill Clinton—but not all of them and it doesn't really matter.

When I began, I closed my eyes and reached out to all of the "greats" of speaking and invited them to contribute to creating this book. I explained that I have some good ideas but I don't know everything that they know and will they contribute their energy to this book, its life and to what it can create in the world.

The way that it has been working for me is, I chose to write and have become aware of certain things. I get an insight, an idea or a topic that I may not have considered or been aware of before and rush to find pen and paper to note it down. When I am next at the computer, I pull out those notes and begin typing. Within several hours there is a new chapter looking back at me from the screen. Each time I open that chapter to review it or proofread, I discover further explanation or detail hidden in amongst the existing words and can expand and refine the piece. My choice of writing up that topic seems to create more of it being available to me. Rarely do I know where the writing is leading to, but I'm frequently delighted with where we go—it is an adventure with writing.

You can do something similar and enhance the way you speak or perform. Let me give you an example.

Blossom Benedict is a terrific singer and coach. Blossom presents classes worldwide that assist people in various areas of performance; though she uses singing as her main platform. I participated in her class in Costa Rica, several years ago.

> Blossom invited one member of the audience to come up on stage and sing. Birgitta chose a children's song that she remembered singing when she was young and had sung with her own children. As she faced her audience she had a bright pink flush to her cheeks, laughed a lot, forgot the words,

did some deep breathing and managed to get through it. She sang in her native Swedish and most of us didn't understand the words, but it was fine.

After the applause died down Blossom came over and whispered in Birgitta's ear, covering with her hand, so we couldn't hear and then asked the Swede to sing again. The difference was amazing.

Birgitta closed her eyes for a moment and then began. She sang with a child-like vulnerability, which tugged at my heart. The buzz of excited audience energy quickly disappeared and everyone became quiet and present with Birgitta, and the song. Her voice steadied, there was no more nervous laughing and she shared more than words and music. It was a very beautiful and credible performance.

Later, I asked Blossom what she had whispered to Birgitta. She told me she had asked the singer to expand out, beyond the room, and connect with all of the children, over decades, who enjoyed singing that song…and to sing from *that* energy. Birgitta was then able to bring a different energy to the song and facilitate her audience (who still didn't understand one word) to have a different experience. Even though only one voice was heard, it seemed that everyone was singing and there were several damp eyes when she was done—joyful tears. It was quite remarkable.

When you are willing to ask-for and receive beyond your own experience then you have access to so much more to create with. Whether it is simply asking a

Advanced Speaking Concepts

friend to hear and discuss your speech or reaching out to energies unknown, you are inviting contribution and that can facilitate you in being greater.

> What energies are available in the world that you can connect-with and speak-from?

And remember, just because you cannot see it or touch it doesn't mean that it doesn't exist.

When a person or persons create something that has not existed in the world before, the "thing" and its energy becomes available to those who will receive it. Experiments with mice suggest that those who come after the first mouse, who has solved a puzzle, can do it faster and easier. Are they accessing the informational energy created by their predecessors?

My parents have been cumbersome with learning and using computers, while at thirty eight years old I became competent with greater ease. My sister's two boys were mousing around at three years old with no training and had figured out how to crack the family computer's password. What information were they accessing, seemingly, beyond their years?

As a speaker or performer, you can create more, when you consciously access the energies relating to your topic. Just as Birgitta drew upon the joy of children singing, you too can engage the energies of grief, joy, loss, humour and many more to enhance your performance.

And we can use this to create limitation too. I realised, as a child, when I made a decision that speaking-out fearlessly was dangerous, I immediately had access to all of the fear-related energies and information to support and reinforce my decision. As a young child I didn't have the actual experience of making a public speech and being fearful of it, I had to get that particular information from outside of my own experience and apply it in whatever naïve way I could.

Unconsciousness is a barrier we use to *not* have access to everything that is available to us. Being conscious or aware of these possibilities gives us all greater choice.

Exclusion

What Can You Add?

Be aware of who you exclude by your choices of who you include.

A friend who is a teacher, after reading a draft of *Advanced Speaking Concepts*, related the following story.

> "Each year, my school has a touring theatre troupe perform for about 200 students. This year, a troupe did a great story about teenage issues (performance anxiety, peer and school stress). My observations, from the back of the room, were that the actors:
>
> - seemed to be in their own bubble in the stage area
> - knew the script and displayed great emotion through body movement
> - did not engage the whole audience, only about the first four to five rows
> - did not use enough voice projection or energy
>
> The audience, beyond rows four and five were confused and felt left out. These students had no clue of what the performance was about.
>
> It took a lot of work and energy on my part,

to control the students and keep them from disengaging totally (behavior management).

I realized that the actors inability, or unwillingness to engage the whole audience had the effect of excluding most of the students."—Simone Phillips, Dip. Teach.

When you exclude some portion of your audience, you force them to try reaching for you. It is very difficult for an audience to get your attention as they have few tools available; audiences are supposed to sit quietly and listen to you, the great speaker. Unconsciously they will begin to fidget, yawn and perhaps even get up and leave.

Those actors were not being big enough to fill the whole room with their presence and fully engage every student. They were used to smaller audiences and kept their energy at that familiar level. It was not enough.

Great speakers and performers fill all the space; they are everywhere; there is no space they are not. As a result, every person in the audience feels connected to them, engaged by them and a part of the whole of them.

Larger audiences demand more of a speaker. They demand that the speaker connect with them all, from those seated in the first row to the very last person in the last row.

Do not make the mistake of excluding people by the people you include. Expand you to fill all the space and to be all the space so that no one in your audience is excluded from your presence.

The famous 1960s musician Jimi Hendrix and his band

The Jimi Hendrix Experience used powerful, overdriven Marshall amplifiers and large speakers to fill even the farthest corners of auditoriums with their music; and the audiences they played for demanded and loved them for it.

> "Rock is so much fun. That's what it's all about - filling up the chest cavities and empty kneecaps and elbows."—Jimi Hendrix

Certain mannerisms, learned behaviors or habits can be used by a speaker to unconsciously include some members of the audience, and effectively exclude others.

At a 2014 National Press Club (Australia) speech, Universities Australia chair Professor Sandra Harding spoke from a written speech. She glanced from her notes, repeatedly up and to the left several times and then up and to the right. It was most noticeable and worked to exclude the whole centre section of the audience. She had developed a habitual, repetitive movement designed to create eye contact with the audience that in practice seemed unnatural, even robotic.

Some speakers who work from written speeches look up and down so quickly that it is unlikely that their eyes have time to focus. The audience must appear to them as a blur of indistinct shapes, lights and shadows; and for the audience, it may be a very disconcerting experience.

Creating Inclusion

Written speeches are a part of the work a speaker may be engaged in and there are many techniques that can assist in creating a more inclusive and natural performance. Here's a small selection:

1. Learn how to read forward, ahead of what is coming out of your mouth. In this way you can look to your audience for longer periods of time before fixing back on the writing.

2. Slow your rate of speech down and pause often (natural speech includes lots of pauses), to give you time to anticipate appropriate gestures or movement.

3. Build-in sections to your written speech where you know you can ad lib confidently, and "eyeball" the audience for minutes at a time; perhaps speaking directly to individual people.

4. Watch videos of your speeches and review what you can change or do differently, then practice those things.

5. Ask your audience questions; even rhetorical questions allow you to pause and look around the room.

6. In your written speech, highlighted in the text, write *yourself* questions and respond to them as if an audience member had asked, speaking spontaneously.

There is a great deal of information available to assist you in polishing your speaking performance. Research what is available, try it and choose what works for you.

Seek to become aware of what you are doing and what it creates for both you and your audience. You may find, often, that it is not about trying to fix that "particular" technique or thing, or getting rid of it. It may be much easier to simply add more to your repertoire; more for you to choose from and to work with. In the game of golf, many amateur players are obsessed with getting rid of their "slice" or "hook" shot. There are times, though, that hooking the ball around a tree can be very useful. Rather than getting rid of these shots they can work to *add more* shots, for example, a straight shot and a short shot; which would give them more shots to choose from when playing.

> What else can you add to your speaking and speeches that you have not considered before?

As you add more to your speaking, you will find that you are including more of your audience in your speeches. And when you are willing to be totally inclusive, the contribution an audience can be to you may suprise you.

Applause

A Beginning

Applause is often viewed as signaling the end of a speech or performance, but it is this view that limits future possibilities between a speaker and their audience. What if applause was a beginning, hopefully one of many, that activates what else is to come; what else is possible?

When applause is created as an ending, then there is no "what else." An ending excludes future possibility by its very nature, "end, conclusion, boundary." What you create with your speech, that has been contributed-to by the audience, now has energy; a life-force of its own that will expand and grow if you nurture it, rather than end it.

Relationships & Connections

What is it that you facilitate for your audience during a speech? When you get up on stage, you allow an audience to judge you. Many speakers (and individuals) see judgement as a bad thing; something to be avoided at all costs. You need to understand what your audience is really doing or it may, indeed, cost you. It is by their judgement that they can create relationship with you; relate to you and you have a large part to play in the judgements they come up with.

> "…every relationship you had was created based on judgment."—Gary Douglas, author of Divorceless Relationships.

It is through relationship that many people can feel connected. Relationship is a, "sense or state of being related." Relation, "connected."

In this book and in *Public Speaking: Beyond Fear*, I've written extensively about creating a connection with your audience that will allow them to accept and trust you more easily. It is through the relationship *they* create with you, one you nurture and grow, that their connection to you may be achieved. Applause can be the beginning of that relationship.

It is with applause that an audience can, "express agreement or approval; to praise." To be approved-of, implies that you have been "tried or tested (to find if it is good)."

So, applause may be described as that which signifies you passing the test and being judged genuine; the real thing, and whatever is next can now begin.

Your Part

It may surprise you to know that you contribute to the judgements that other people have of you; some people say that we actually create those judgements. The way you look, dress, speak, walk and behave will create others judging you.

People judge; it's a given, especially for a speaker or performer who may be in front of large groups of people. Your ability to allow their judgements, without having to do anything with them, will go a long way to nurturing the relationship audiences may desire to have with you.

Allowance is not compromise, it is not tolerance; it is *you* allowing others to have their view; their opinion without judging them for it.

What great allowance are you really capable of?

There are other aspects to applause, relating to the gift you are to an audience when you fully receive their applause, and I discuss this in *Public Speaking: Beyond Fear*. My target here is to connect you with the concept of a beginning—applause as the beginning of what can come, generated by you with your talk or event.

In the same sense, as we come to the end of this book, is it really an end or is it a beginning? This is something for you dear reader. Do you applaud or boo and hiss? Did I pass the test or not? What connection did we create and what future possibilities can now come into our worlds?

As a writer I will not hear your response but as a speaker, one day I may and that will be fun. I wish you well with your speaking; may every success be yours, and I encourage you to enjoy the continuing adventure that awaits you with every new choice you make.

One More Thing
A favour, please.

If you got anything from this book; highlighted something, scribbled a note or took a quote then give this copy to someone else.

Ask them to read it and make a choice about public speaking.

Imagine, even if they only read the chapter "Speak or Die" and then gave up their view that public speaking is something to be feared. What might that change in the world? What could *that* choice create?

And remember, **choice creates**; your choice here creates.

Stephen Outram

About The Author

Biography

Stephen Outram has a background of some 18 years in architecture, and since 1997 has worked as a graphic artist, website developer and Internet consultant. More recently he has written several books, spoken and presented seminars on a number of topics.

Educated in Queensland, Australia, Stephen studied at Brisbane's University of Technology in the 1970s. He returned to study in 1995 at Dundee University, Scotland, achieving a Master of Science degree in Computing.

Stephen was an active member of Toastmasters where he became President of Gold Coast Toastmasters Club, representing the club in speaking competitions and official events.

He is author of several books and numerous Internet articles.

His family emigrated to Australia, from the United Kingdom in 1965, originally landing in Freemantle, Western Australia and spending 5 years in the northerly town of Port Hedland. In 1970 the family drove across the country from west to east and settled in Queensland's Gold Coast, where his parents and sister still reside.

Stephen enjoys a diverse and wide range of projects including work, writing, music and song writing, boats and some sport. He is active with Surfrider Foundation Australia and is interested in sustainable and flourishing coastlines and waterways, free of plastics and pollution.

For more information, visit the website:

stephenoutram.com

Related Books

Public Speaking: Beyond Fear

Public Speaking: Beyond Fear is designed for people who experience difficulty with public speaking and performance. It will also benefit people who think they have it all handled.

The ideas, concepts and tools contained in this book may catapult you to levels of freedom and ease with public speaking that you've never had before.

- Begin functioning beyond normal
- Discover why anxiety is your best friend
- The weird, *hidden issues* that you can change
- The Art of Public Speaking explained
- Understanding Fight-Flight and working *with* your body
- Why amateur speakers never get paid

What if your journey with public speaking was really an adventure, unfolding before you with each new choice you make?

More information at stephenoutram.com

Notes

Advanced Speaking Concepts

Stephen Outram

Advanced Speaking Concepts

Stephen Outram

www.ingramcontent.com/pod-product-compliance
Lightning Source LLC
Chambersburg PA
CBHW021025090426
42738CB00007B/907